Emerald Home Lawyer

CONVEYANCING

A Practical Guide
Revised Edition
Peter Wade

Emerald Publishing

© Peter Wade 2015

ISBN: 9781847165855

Printed by 4edge Ltd www.4edge.co.uk

Cover design by Emerald Graphics

Contents

1. Conveyancing of Registered Land

2. Acting for the Seller – Sellers Checklist

3. Exchanging Contracts

4 .Acting for the Purchaser – Purchaser's Checklist

5. Acting for Seller in Freehold and Leasehold matters

6. Acting for Purchaser's

7. Council of Mortgage Lenders Handbook and requirements

8. Completion and post completion

Glossary of Terms

Standard conveyancing letters

Schedule of forms used in conveyancing

Index

****

1

Conveyancing of Registered Land

Outline of a Conveyancing Transaction

A conveyancing transaction breaks down into three stages whether we are dealing with a sale or a purchase.

1. The pre-contract stage.

2. The time between exchange of contracts and completion or pre-completion stage

   and

3. Post-completion stage.

The pre-contract stage is the longest and most complicated (contrary to what estate agents might tell you). Most of the legal work is done at this stage. Once contracts are exchanged things become time critical.

All of the delay takes place up to exchange of contracts and these can be attributable to things such as completing the chain of transactions, local authority searches time for everyone to obtain their mortgages. In a chain of transaction obviously the chain only proceeds at the pace of the slowest party.

OUTLINE OF A SALE

1. Taking instructions

2. Preparing pre-contract package to include office copy entries, fixtures and fittings list, sellers property information form

3. Exchange of Contracts

4. Approve transfer document

5. Answer Completion Information and Requisitions on Title

6. Prepare for completion

7. Completion

8. Post completion matters such as sending deeds to purchaser's solicitors pay off seller's mortgage.

OUTLINE OF PURCHASE

1. Take Instructions

2. Pre-contract searches and enquiries

3. Investigate title

4. Approve draft Contract

5. Exchange Contract

6. Prepare purchase deed

7. Pre completion searches

8. Prepare for completion

9. Complete

10. Post-completion matters such as pay Stamp Duty Land tax, register at land registry.

PRE-COMPLETION STAGE

The seller's solicitors must prepare a pre-completion package for the purchaser's solicitors

This consists of:

1. The draft contract which describes the land that is being sold and the price together with all the other terms of the transaction such as interest rates in the event of late completion, the amount of the deposit etc.

2. Evidence of the seller's title which nowadays usually consists of official office copies of the sellers' title at the land registry together with the filed plan. You can purchase the office copy entries and title plan for a fee on the Land Registry website www.landregistryservices.com

3. Fixtures, fittings and contents list and solicitors property information form.

It may also include copy planning permissions, building regulations consents and guarantees.

Title

This usually consists of the official copies of the entries at the land registry but still may be unregistered title.

Searches

Any number of searches may be obtained but the essential pre contract searches would be a local land charge search.

Other optional search's might be:

Water search

Environmental search

Mining search

Radon gas search

Finances

Most purchasers proceed with a mortgage provided by a bank or a building society.

Normally some sort of deposit is required, formerly ten-percent but now usually by negotiation.

The purchaser and his solicitor would need to be satisfied that sufficient funds are available to complete the purchase before contracts are exchanged.

Draft contract

This is the most important part of the transaction. Once the purchasers' solicitors are happy with the draft contract, it can then be prepared for exchange of contracts. The purchasers and sellers sign contracts in exactly the same format and they each sign their respective parts.

Once they are ready the solicitor will exchange the contract with a deposit changing hands.

Exchange of Contracts

This creates a binding contract. Neither party can then go back on the agreement without severe financial penalties.

Up until this point either party may withdraw from the transaction without any penalty.

There are various methods of exchanging contracts which have been developed by solicitors. There are various formulae, A, B and C being the most commonly used because it is a telephone exchange of contracts which requires the deposit is sent immediately thereafter.

Much confusion surrounds the deposit. It is a part payment towards the purchase price and a form of security. The deposit will be forfeited if the purchaser withdraws. It is usually held by one of the solicitors as stakeholder which means it belongs to neither party until some other event happens such a completion.

Builders usually insist that their solicitors hold the deposit as agents' for the vendor. This has the risk that if the builder goes bust before completion that the purchaser may have lost his deposit, but once contracts are exchanged the purchaser may have a legitimate claim to the property.

From a legal and financial point of view exchange of contracts is the most important part of the transaction. As finances should have been set up completion is more of a practical part of the transaction that is the changing of funds and the moving in of the parties.

Post-Exchange of Contracts

Traditionally the purchasers' solicitor's raises requisitions on title. In the days of unregistered title this was a more onerous activity than nowadays. It should be an administrative matter to enquire as to the amount required at completion and where completion is to take place. It also deals with the undertaking to pay off mortgages.

Completion statement

If the property is leasehold then there will be a completion statement as items such as rent, service charge and insurance will need to be apportioned, that is worked out on a daily basis.

The amount required by the seller's solicitors at completion should be checked carefully so as to obviate any problems that an incorrect figure may cause. It is good practice to confirm it in writing and to get the seller's solicitors to agree so as to avoid any shocks or misunderstandings.

The Purchase Deed

Now known as the TR1 for the transfer of the whole of a title which is the most common. This is a printed form which just has to be competed with all the relevant information. A decision has to be made as to whether it should be signed by all the parties. If there is a covenant to observe previous restrictions then both sellers and purchasers need to sign.

It is the purchaser's duty to produce the purchase deed which is usually submitted in duplicate along with the requisitions on title. If approved the draft is used as the top copy. Care should be taken over spelling of names and the price as this is the document that will be submitted to the land registry and the opportunities to amend this document apart from minor amendments will be limited and could cause problems.

The seller must always sign the purchase deed as this is a basic requirement in the transfer of land.

MORTGAGE CONSIDERATIONS

The purchasers' solicitor is usually instructed by the lender to prepare the mortgage and obtain a good and marketable title for the lender. The lender secures his lending against the title by way of a legal mortgage. This is evidenced by the purchaser signing a mortgage deed and this being registered at the land registry as a charge.

The property cannot be sold without this charge being paid off. Lenders will normally only want and insist upon a first legal charge. This means they will have the right to enforce their charge by selling the property as mortgagee in possession in the event of the mortgage not being repaid.

In exchange for this the lender advances the money on the security of the property and the purchaser's solicitors' job is to make sure the funds are there at completion. The purchasers' solicitor will have to comply with all the conditions in the mortgage and submit a report on title. Once this has been accepted the funds will be available to complete

The purchasers' solicitors will have to undertake an extra search on behalf of the lender which is a bankruptcy search confirming the purchaser is not bankrupt.

PREPARING FOR COMPLETION

Prior to completion the final searches have to be undertaken which includes the bankruptcy search on behalf of the lender and a search of the title. This is a OS1 search which confirms that there have been no changes since the official copies were produced.

It has the second most important effect of giving the purchaser and his lender a priority period. This means during this period which will usually extend for at least thirty days no one else can register anything against this title.

During the period which should extend way beyond completion the purchaser should arranged for the stamp duty to be paid, the title to be registered at the land registry.

This is one of the most important aspects of searches, the priority periods and they should be noted in the diary carefully. Protection ends when the property period expires and you are taking a risk if you exceed the period as some other event can take place such as someone else registering a charge or any other kind of entry.

Discharge of sellers' Mortgage.

Most sellers have mortgages and this will need to be cleared on completion. The seller's solicitors will obtain the redemption figure that is the figure to clear the mortgage on completion.

Once this has been ascertained it is usually paid off on completion by telegraphic transfer. The seller's solicitors give an undertaking to do this and provide in due course either an END being a electronic notification of discharge or DS1 which is a paper discharge that needs to be lodged with the purchase document at the land registry

COMPLETION

These days this is a paperwork exercise technically the completion takes place at the sellers solicitors office where the balance of the purchase price is exchanged for the transfer deed, the discharge of the mortgage or an undertaking thereof any other title deeds and the keys.

The sellers solicitor undertakes that on receipt of the funds through the banking system that they will

1. Arrange for release of the keys which are usually held by the seller's estate agent.

2. Will date and forward the executed transfer deed.

3. Arrange to discharge the seller's mortgage

4. Give the purchasers solicitors an undertaking that the mortgage will be discharged.

5. Give a clear title to the purchaser that is discharge any other items on the title such as giving a clear receipt for any apportionments etc.

Clients think they have to attend completion but they need to be giving vacant possession of their existing property and taking possession of their new property. They will be informed by telephone of the transaction.

POST COMPLETION

Sellers Solicitors

1. Must redeem his client's mortgage.

2. Must obtain from the lender a receipt which he must send to the purchasers solicitors to show it has been redeemed either at END or DS1.

3. Pay any balance back to his client.

4. It is traditional that the seller's solicitor pays the estate agents commission account.

Buyers Solicitor

Prior to completion the purchasers solicitor must obtain a form being a stamp duty land tax form signed by the purchaser stating what, if any, stamp duty land tax should be paid. This must be submitted to the Inland Revenue whether duty is payable or not.

Stamp duty rates

The SDLT rates for residential properties changed on 4 December 2014. The current rates and thresholds are shown below.

If you exchanged contracts on or before 3 December 2014 and completed on 4 December 2014 or later, you can choose to pay SDLT at the old or new rates.

SDLT rates and thresholds for residential properties

SDLT is charged at increasing rates for each portion of the purchase price.

Property purchase price	SDLT rate from 4 December 2014
Up to £125,000	Zero
The next £125,000 (the portion from £125,001 to £250,000)	2%
The next £675,000 (the portion from £250,001 to £925,000)	5%
The next £575,000 (the portion from £925,001 to £1.5 million)	10%
The remaining amount (the portion above £1.5 million)	12%

Example

A buyer exchanges contracts for the purchase of a house for £275,000 on 5 December 2014, with completion expected in February 2015. The SDLT on the property is calculated as follows.

Charge	Amount
0% on the first £125,000 (a)	£0
2% on the next £125,000 (b)	£2,500
5% on the final £25,000 (c)	£1,250
Total SDLT (a + b + c)	£3,750

Residential leaseholds

If you buy a new residential leasehold, SDLT is payable on both the:

- purchase price (lease premium) - use the current SDLT residential rates

- 'net present value' (NPV) of the rent payable

14

The NPV is based on the value of the total rent over the life of the lease.

NPV of rent (residential)	SDLT rate
£0 to £125,000	Zero
The portion over £125,000	1%

Corporate bodies

SDLT is charged at 15% on residential properties costing more than £500,000 bought by certain corporate bodies (or 'non-natural persons'). These include:

- companies

- partnerships including companies

- collective investment schemes

The 15% rate doesn't apply to property bought by trustees of a settlement or bought by a company to be used for:

- a property rental business

- property developers and trader

- property made available to the public

- financial institutions acquiring property in the course of lending

- property occupied by employees

- farmhouses

The standard residential rate of SDLT applies in these cases. These exclusions are subject to specific conditions.

Buying 6 or more residential properties in one transaction

If 6 or more properties form part of a single transaction the rules, rates and thresholds for non-residential properties apply.

The amounts paid for all the properties in the transaction must be added together to establish the SDLT payable.

Non-residential and mixed use properties

Non-residential property includes:

- commercial property such as shops or offices

- agricultural land

- forests

- any other land or property which is not used as a dwelling

- 6 or more residential properties bought in a single transaction

A mixed use property is one that incorporates both residential and non-residential elements.

SDLT rates and thresholds for sales and transfers on new non-residential or mixed use land or property

The rates below apply to freehold and leasehold non-residential and mixed use purchases and transfers.

Purchase price/lease premium or transfer value	SDLT rate
Up to £150,000 - if annual rent is under £1,000	Zero
Up to £150,000 - if annual rent is £1,000 or more	1%
£150,001 to £250,000	1%
£250,001 to £500,000	3%

Purchase price/lease premium or transfer value	SDLT rate
Over £500,000	4%

The annual rent is the highest annual rent known to be payable in any year of the lease, not the NPV used to determine any tax payable on the rent.

SDLT rates and thresholds for rent on new non-residential or mixed use land or property

If you buy a new non-residential or mixed use leasehold property, SDLT is payable on both the:

- lease premium or purchase price

- NPV of the rent payable

These are calculated separately and then added together.

NPV of rent	SDLT rate
£0 - £150,000	Zero
The portion of the value over £150,000	1%

Application must be made to the land registry to register the transaction.

This will involve sending:

1. The fee

2. The transfer TR1

3. Evidence of any previous mortgage being paid off

4. Details of the new charge by delivery of a copy of the mortgage and the original mortgage.

The title can then be registered in the name of the new purchaser together with any charge.

Once registration is completed a copy should be sent to the purchaser for checking and any original documents should be sent to the lender for safekeeping.

Since the advent of dematerialization of title deeds the need for title deeds has decreased. This is because registration at the Land Registry has proved title in and of itself and no deeds are required to prove ownership. The lender will be satisfied to receive a copy of the Office Copy Entries, which show the new charges register which is part C of the Office Copy entries, which will show there is a charge listed.

SALE AND PURCHASE.

Most transactions involve a sale and purchase.

Obviously the money from the purchase is tied up in the sale. All the above sale and purchase procedures need to be undertaken but all simultaneously that is why it is vital to have a foolproof method of exchanging contracts to make sure there are no hitches.

The National Conveyancing Protocol.

This was introduced in 1990 and was intended to standardise simplify and speed up domestic conveyancing transactions.

The protocol forms have already been mentioned such as fixtures fittings and contents form and seller's property information form. Also there is a standard form of contract.

LEGAL BACKGROUND TO CONVEYANCING

First Registration

1) First registration must take place within two months of new triggers, first registration being amongst other things:

   a) Deeds of Gift

   b) Conveyances and Assignments

   c) First Mortgagees

   d) Assents

   e) Vesting Assents

The Land Registry have issued a practice advice leaflet (No.14) which contains detailed guidance of these triggers.

The only estates capable of registration are freehold and leasehold titles.

All leases over 7 years are registerable leases, and should be registered at the Land Registry.

Classes of Registered Title

- **Freehold absolute** – this is the best class of Title available. The Titleholder will take the legal estate, subject to any encumbrances protected by an entry on the register and overriding interest.

- **Freehold Possessory** – the registrar is not satisfied with the applicant's title, possessory title will be issued. The proprietor will take subject to any adverse interest, which exist or are capable of existing at the date of the first registration.

- **Freehold Qualified** – this title is very rare. It is for freehold land where there is defect or flaw affecting the applicant's title.

- **Leasehold Absolute** – This is for a term of years equivalent to the freehold absolute class. If an unregistered lease with more than 7 years to run is assigned for value or by gift, it will be the subject of compulsory first registration.

- **Leasehold Possessory** – subject to any estate of interest that is adverse to the proprietor's title at the time of first registration.

- **Leasehold qualified** - the registrar believes that there is a flaw or defect in the leasehold title.

- **Good leasehold** – the registration is such that there is no guarantee that the lease has been invalidly granted, this will be issued when the registrar has not seen the superior title. The problem for this of course is that if the lease is held to be invalid, the lender will lose its security.

Preliminary matters – taking instructions

You should take as detailed instructions as possible at the outset. Constantly asking the client further questions undermines their confidence.

Tax and Planning Consequences

By obtaining full instructions other matters can be taken into account such as:

- Insuring the property

- Inheritance tax

- Co-ownership

- Planning

Take instructions in person where possible, in a personal interview.

Co-Sellers

Authority should be obtained from any co-seller or purchaser.

Status of the Conveyancer

The status of the conveyancer should be confirmed to the client and details of the complaints procedure given.

Protocol Forms

- Property Information Form (2nd Edition)

- Fixtures Fittings and Contents (2nd Edition)

- Leasehold Information Form (2nd Edition)

These should be completed

Financial Charges

Details of all second and subsequent mortgages, improvement grants, discounts payable to the local authority and any other residents of the property should be established. Client care letters should be sent, giving estimate of charges etc.

Lender's requirements

Identity: the client must be verified in accordance with the Council of Mortgage Lenders Handbook. Taking any specific instructions to be included as special conditions.

Planning

The client should be asked the proposed use of the property, as it might require planning permission or affect restrictive covenants.

Tax

Does the transaction attract Capital Gains Tax, advise the client accordingly.

****

2

Acting For The Seller

Sellers Checklist

- Client – full names and addresses of sellers, buyers home and business telephone numbers

- Estate agents details

- Where are the Title Deeds?

- Client's authority to obtain them

- Full address of the property

- Price

- Deposits

- Fixtures and Fittings

- Are they being removed?

- Any instructions on completion date

- Various use of the premises

- Who is resident at the premises

- Dependant on a purchase?

- Any other special conditions

- Any tenancy

- Advice as to Costs

- Any outstanding mortgages

- Where the proceeds of sale are to go

- Any C G T on sale proceeds

- Does it have to be synchronised with any other related purchase

- Obtain answers to Sellers Property Information Form and Fixtures, Fittings and Contents

- Check Identity of Client

SALES CONSIDERATIONS

- Request Title Deeds

- Request Office Copy Entries

- Draft Contract.

STANDARD CONDITIONS OF SALE (Fifth Edition)

Formerly contracts were headed Agreement, as we use terms like Exchange of Contracts, the word Agreement has been deleted.

Standard conditions of the contract normally incorporate the Standard Conditions of Sale either the 4th or 5th edition.

The Seller is to transfer the property with either full title guarantee or limited title guarantee, as specified on the front page of the Contract.

Standard conditions of sale set out all aspects of the transaction and the formation of the contract:

- Deposit

- Matters affecting the property

- Physical state

- Title and Transfer

Deposit

The buyer is to pay or send a deposit of 10% of the total of the purchase price and the Chattels price no later than the date of the contract.

Matters affecting the property

The property is sold free from encumbrances, other than those mentioned in the contract, those discoverable by inspection; those are available for inspection in the public register.

Physical State

The Buyer accepts the property in the physical state it is in at the date of the contract unless the seller is building or converting it.

Title and Transfer

The condition sets out how the seller will deduce title to both registered and unregistered land

Requisitions

The buyer may be precluded from raising requisitions on items that have been disclosed prior to exchange of contracts

Commonhold

This is under the Commonhold and Leasehold format 2002.The seller must provide a copy of the memorandum and articles of the common holders association and of the Commonhold community statement.

The front page of the contract sets out the sellers and buyers names.

The description of the property whether it is freehold or leasehold and its postal address.

Title number or Root of Title

Any specified Incumbrances

Title Guarantee – whether full or limited

When it has full title guarantee the seller has the right to dispose of the property and will at their own expense, make every reasonable effort to transfer the title offered, and the seller transfers free of all charges and incumbrances.

Limited title guarantee states that the transferor has not himself or herself encumbered the property and is not aware that anyone else has. An example of this would be a personal representative.

In leasehold titles both full and limited title guarantee imply that the lease is subsisting and that there is no existing breach that might result in forfeiture.

A plan is usually necessary for either transfer of whole or transfer of part, obviously more easily obtained now that most properties are registered. It is possible to obtain a plan from the Land Registry by asking on the Index map search and this plan can be agreed for the transfer and the contract.

Sending the papers to the Purchaser Solicitors

- Draft contract in duplicate – you are recommended to keep you own file copy.

- The Protocol forms- Fixtures, Fittings and Contents, and Property Information Form

For Leasehold title, you would normally include

- Last service charge and three years accounts.

- Copy of Share Certificate of Management Company

- Copy of memorandum and articles of association

- Copy of block insurance policy and schedule

- Any guarantees, damp, timber, preservation etc

- Any copy of planning permission as building regulation consent

Further enquiries from purchaser's solicitors.

It is recommended that you take the client's express instructions concerning any replies to further enquiries.

The client will be liable for any misrepresentation in giving the reply.

If there has been any breach of planning or building regulation consent it is possible to obtain an indemnity.

Receiving Draft Contract

- Report to client on contract and obtain their execution thereto

- Confirm price, chattels, rates of interest etc with client.

If appropriate obtain client's instructions concerning a date for completion.

****

3

Exchange of Contracts

The Law Society's Formulae

Once the purchaser's and sellers are ready to exchange the buyer's solicitor indicates that the seller is now ready to commit to a binding contract.

Obviously once contracts have been exchanged, neither party will be able to withdraw from the contract, and therefore all documents and arrangements will need to be checked thoroughly.

If there is a dependant sale the solicitor must ensure that the exchange of contracts on both properties is synchronised to avoid leaving his client either owning two houses or being homeless.

If there is a failure of synchronisation it could be professional negligence.

Telephone

Exchange of contracts by telephone is the most common method of effecting an exchange.

Apart from a personal exchange no other method is entirely risk free. If contracts are exchanged at the telephone then the telephone conversation is the confirmation of exchange of contracts.

To avoid all uncertainties, the Law Society has agreed various formulae.

The most important aspect of using any of the formulae is an accurate attendance note recording the telephone conversation must be made as soon as practicable.

A typical memorandum of exchange would include:

- Date

- Time

- Wording of any variations

- Identity of any parties to the conversation.

- Purchase price - agree Deposit

Any variation of the formulae, such as reduced deposit, must be expressly agreed and noted in writing.

Law Society Formula A

This is for use when one solicitor holds both signed parts of the Contract.

The parties agree that exchange will take place from that moment and the solicitor holding both parts confirms that he or she undertakes by first class post or DX to send his or her signed part of the contract to the other solicitor, together with deposit as appropriate.

Law Society Formula B

For use where each solicitor holds his own client's signed part of the contract.

- Each solicitor confirms to the other that he or she holds the signed part of the agreed form signed by the clients, and will forthwith insert the agreed completion date

- Each solicitor undertakes to send by first class post or DX his or her signed part of the contract to the other together with the deposit if appropriate.

Law Society Formula C

Part 1

Each solicitor confirms that he or she holds the part of the contract in agreed form signed by his or her client,

Each solicitor undertakes to the other that, they will hold that part of the contract until part 2 of the formula takes place.

Part 2

Each solicitor undertakes to hold part of the contract in his or her possession to the other's order, so that contracts are exchanged at that moment and to send it to the other on that day.

This is effectively the giving and receiving of a release, which is as important as exchanging contracts.

The parties have to comply with the release within the agreed time frame.

When synchronising you normally arrange to receive a release on your sales transaction from your buyer's solicitor, with say a time up to which it is effective.

When you have received your release on your sale you then give a release on your related purchase, with a slightly shorter time frame to allow you to exchange on the original transaction.

When your seller exchanges with you within the time that you have given to release you then go to your purchaser and exchange within the time on the release given to you.

It is obviously essential to make sure that once you have exchanged on your sale that you immediately exchange on purchase.

It is very important to have the terms of the release noted as carefully as if you were exchanging contracts, because one more phone call will then create an exchange of contract.

Client Care

Solicitors' Costs. Information and Client Care Code

The Client must be given cost information which must not be inaccurate or misleading, clearly in a way and a level which is appropriate to that particular client.

It should be confirmed in writing to the client as soon as possible. The basis of the firm's charges should be explained.

The solicitor should keep the client properly informed about costs as the matter progresses. The solicitor should tell the client, how much the costs are at regular intervals, like at least every six months and in appropriate cases delivering handbills at agreed intervals.

Complaints handling

The client must be told the name of the person in the firm to contact about any problems with the service provided.

The firm must have a written complaints procedure to ensure that the complaints are handled in accordance with it and ensure the client is given a copy of the complaints procedure on request.

Stamp Duty Land Tax

The full rates of tax were outlined in chapter 2. The basic rates of Tax are: (overleaf)

Property purchase price	SDLT rate from 4 December 2014
Up to £125,000	Zero
The next £125,000 (the portion from £125,001 to £250,000)	2%
The next £675,000 (the portion from £250,001 to £925,000)	5%
The next £575,000 (the portion from £925,001 to £1.5 million)	10%
The remaining amount (the portion above £1.5 million)	12%

Who should complete the Land Transaction Return?

It is the responsibility of the purchaser to make sure the information contained in the return is complete and correct, and is the purchaser who must sign the declaration on the return SDLT1.

Type of Property

Types of property are residential, mixed or non- residential. Description of transaction: every acquisition of a freehold or leasehold interest in land is included within this, but it also includes a contract or agreement for the acquisition of an interest where that contract is substantially performed.

Effective date of transaction.

The effective date will be the completion date or the earlier date of substantial performance.

About the Tax Calculation

There are designated disadvantaged areas and they will have a nil rate up to £150,000.

There is no need to forward the transfer or document of transfer, it is a tax on a transaction. There may not be in fact any document giving effect of the transaction.

It is a self-assessed tax and the burden of calculating any tax falls on the payer.

Whether or not any tax is payable a Land Transaction return in the appropriate form must be submitted to the revenue within 30 days of the chargeable event.

There are fines thereafter.

Sending in the return

Once the return is sent in and is correct a certificate will be issued.

This certificate will enable you to register the transaction with the Land Registry

****

4

Acting for the Purchaser-Purchasers Transaction Checklist

BUYERS CHECKLIST

- Existing client?

- Full names and address of the clients

- Estate agents details

- Freehold or Leasehold

- Price

- Any preliminary deposit paid

- Any fixtures and fittings being removed

- Any instructions on completion date

- Present or proposed use of the property

- Who is resident at the property

- How will any deposit be funded

- How is the balance of the purchase price to be funded – that is has the client obtained a mortgage

- Survey arrangements – is the property being surveyed?

- Give advice of types of survey

- How Is the property to be held – joint tenants or tenants in common

- Check clients identity in accordance with the CML handbook

****

5

Acting for the Seller in Freehold and Leasehold Matters

Sales transaction checklist – Sale of property-leasehold and freehold

- Seller

- Purchaser

- Purchasers solicitors

- Completion date.

1)   Take full instructions from client

2)   Obtain Title Deeds/Official copies of the Register

3)   Have Protocol Forms, property information and fixture, fittings and contents to be completed by client

4)   Send draft contract – Official copies of the Register – protocol forms to purchasers solicitors

5)   Obtain approval of draft contract from purchaser's solicitors

6)   Obtain and have contract signed by client

7)   Exchange contracts

8)   Request redemption figures for all charges on the property

9)   Obtain estate agent's commission account

10)   Reply to requisitions on title and approve draft transfer

11)   Prepare bill and financial statement once the estate agents fee and redemption figure have been received

12)   Obtain signature to the transfer

Completion

a) Forward a transfer and DS1/END to purchasers solicitors

b) Redeem existing mortgages either by cheque or CHAPS

c) Pay estate agent's account

d) Account for proceeds of sales to client

e) Receive DS1/END from mortgagee and forward to purchaser's solicitors in accordance with undertaking

****

6

Acting for the Purchasers of Freehold and Leasehold property

Purchase transaction checklist – Purchase of leasehold/freehold

- Purchaser

- Seller

- Completion date

- Take instructions

- Obtain funds for Local Authority search

- Water search

- Environmental search

- Receive the contract

- Protocol forms received

- Send local authority search

- Send environmental search

- Send water search

- Receive mortgage instructions

- Check conditions etc

- Report to client and obtain signature to contract

- Execution of mortgage

- Arrange completion date

- Exchange contracts

- Send report on title to lender

- Insure property

- Start any life policy necessary

- Raise requisitions and draft transfer

- Obtain execution of the transfer and forward to sellers solicitors

- Prepare bill and financial statements

- Send final searches OSI/ K16

- Receive any balance of purchase of monies required

- Receive mortgage advance

- Complete

- Pay Stamp Duty and forward SDLT form

- Once END/DS1 received, register at Land Registry

- Give notice of assignment of any lease if leasehold

- Completion of registration and forward Title Deeds to building society of if no mortgage to client

PURCHASERS IN FREEHOLD AND LEASEHOLD TRANSACTIONS

Receiving Draft paperwork

- Send copy plan to client

Checking

- Check main points of contract with client i.e. price, names to go in the contract

Searches

- Obtain fees from clients for searches being:

- Local search

- Environmental search

- Water search

- Coal mining search if necessary

- Commons registration search

When buying outside your area ask seller's solicitor's what are the usual searches?

- Local land charge search – this will reveal

   a) Planning permissions

   b) Buildings regulation consent

   c) If road adopted

   d) Any road proposals

   e) Any enforcement or planning notices

- Environmental search

- Coal search will reveal whether it is a coal mining area

Raising any preliminary enquiries

Official copy entries to the Title

- You should check

  a) Description of the land according to the contract description

  b) Title number

  c) Estate – freehold or leasehold

  d) Easements

  e) Any rights of way

  f) Flying freeholds

Proprietorship register

- Is the class of Title correct

- Is the seller the registered proprietor

- Any cautions or other entries on the Title

- Undertaking or release of the caution will be required

- Note any restrictive covenants referred to on the Title and advise the client, as this may affect their use and enjoyment of the premises. There may be covenants not to erect anything on the premises without the original owners consent

- Any missing covenants then consider an indemnity

- Any recent sales of the property as an under-value or no value.

- Consider insolvency of seller

Contract/ Agreement

- Check the name of the seller is the same as the proprietorship register

- Similarly Title number

- Check special conditions

Protocol Forms

- Fixtures fitting and contents – this is usually an extra to the contract to incorporate the chattels.

- Obtain client's approval of this prior to exchange of contracts

- Sellers Property Information Form (SPIF) check

  a) Boundaries

  b) Any guarantees

  c) Occupiers

  d) Any changes to the property for planning purposes

  e) Any disputes

Leasehold sellers

- Leasehold information form

- Leasehold enquiries - assignment of lease. The information required by the purchaser's solicitors is similar to a freehold transaction, with the additional details of the lease to be bought.

Items to be checked

- Landlord's consent required

- Length of the residue of term to be checked

- The lender may have specific requirements

- Check plan accurately identifies the property

- Any restrictions on sub-letting i.e. last 7 years

- Does the description of the property conform with the plan

- Does the assignee have to enter into a direct covenant with the landlord. Are there covenants to enforce on behalf of the landlord

- Any covenants against the other tenants

- Check insurance complies with the lenders requirements

- Check service charge accounts for the last three years including receipt for the last sum payable.

- Request whether there is any potential change in the next year.

- Obtain receipt from last rent – similarly service charge

- Check whether any apportionment required

- Check whether any alterations to the premises, which would require landlords, consent.

7

Council Of Mortgage Lenders Handbook(CML Handbook)

The lender's handbook provides comprehensive instructions for conveyancers acting on behalf of lenders in residential conveyancing transactions. It is divided into two parts:

Part 1 sets out the main instructions

Part 2 details each lenders specific requirements relating to the main instructions. (last updated 13th October 2003).

There is a chance of a conflict of interest because you are acting for both the borrower and the lender. If there is any conflict of interest you should refuse to act for one or other of the parties.

You can only reveal information to the lender if the borrower agrees, if the borrower refuses to agree you must return mortgage instructions to the lender.

Communications

All communications with the lender must be in writing, quoting the mortgage account or roll number and the clients name etc.

Safeguards

• A proof of identity of borrowers

• You must follow the guidance of the Law Society's green card (mortgage fraud) and pink card (undertakings under Money Laundering Regulations 1993)

- Proof of identity can be one from List A and two from List B

- List A – valid full passport – valid HM Forces identity card – valid UK Photocard – Driving Licence – any other document in additional list A part two.

- List B – cheques guarantee card- Mastercard or Visa, American Express, Diners Card. All firearms or shotgun certificates or

  a) Receipted utility bill less than three months old

  b) Or council tax bill less than three months old

  c) Rent book

  d) Mortgage statement

Valuation of the property.

The borrower should be advised not to rely upon the report

Re-inspection

Where a final inspection is needed you must ask for the final inspection at least 10 working days before the advance is required.

Title and surrounding circumstances

If the owner or registered proprietor has been registered for less than six months, or if the seller is not the registered proprietor this must be reported unless - the person represented is the registered proprietor of an institution or mortgagee exercising power of sales are receiving bankruptcy, liquidator or developer or builder, selling the property under part exchange scheme.

Searches and reports

You must make all the usual necessary searches and enquiries.

A lender should be named as the applicant in the HM Land Registry search.

All searches except where there is a priority, period must be no more than six months old at completion

All of the searches such as mining searches should be undertaken in the areas affected and for personal searches and search insurance, they should be checked in part two.

Planning and Building Regulations

- The property must have the benefit of any necessary planning consent

- Having a good and marketable title

- The title of the property must be good and marketable, free of any restrictions, covenants, easement, charges or encumbrances, which might reasonably be expected to adversely affect the value of the property.

Flying Freeholds

Freehold flats and other freehold arrangements. Each individual lender will have its own requirements.

Restrictions on use and occupation

Any material restrictions on its use should be reported, such as occupier's employment, age or income.

Restrictive Covenants

You must enquire whether the property is being built, altered or is currently used in breach in of a restrictive covenant.

First Legal Charge

They require a fully enforceable first charge by way of legal mortgage over the property. All existing charges must be redeemed on or before completion.

Leasehold Property

A period of an unexpired lease as set out in part two. There must be no provision for forfeiture on insolvency of the tenant or any superior tenant. There must be satisfactory legal rights for access services, support, shelter and protection.

There must be adequate covenants in respect of building insurance, maintenance, repair of structure, foundations, main walls, roof etc.

You should ensure that responsibility of the insurance, maintenance and repair of the services is through the common services that of the landlord or one or more of the tenants of the building that forms one or more of a management company.

The lease must contain adequate provisions for the enforcement of these obligations of the landlord or Management Company.

If the terms of the lease are unsatisfactory, you must obtain a suitable deed of variation, or indemnity insurance: see part two.

You must obtain on completion the clear receipt or written confirmation of the last payment of ground rent and service charge from the landlord or the managing agent.

Notice of the mortgage must be served on the landlord or any management company.

It must be reported if the landlord is either absent or insolvent

A recent article in the Law Society Gazette stated that a frequent ground for complaint arises when insufficient checks are made by buyer's solicitors to ensure that ground rent, service charges and other outgoings relating to leasehold purchases are paid up to date on completion.

It is both prudent and good practice for the buyer's solicitors to contact the managing agents for the properties directly or to ensure that the seller's solicitors do so.

Solicitors will then be able to ensure that the documentary evidence is available in relation to the payment of ground rents and service charges including apportionment's where appropriate. They can also confirm whether the freehold holder or superior landlord is planning any future improvement or remedial work and can consider the benefit if negotiating a retention with landlord's solicitors to protect their client's. A solicitors omission to seek and to clarify information available from managing agents may result in inadequate professional service.

Management company

The Management Company must have the legal right to enter the property.

You should make a company search and prove that the company is in existence and registered at Company's House.

You should obtain the management companies last three years published accounts.

INSOLVENCY CONSIDERATIONS

You must obtain a clear Bankruptcy search against the borrower.

You must certify that any entries do not relate to the borrower.

If the property is subject to deed of gift or transaction at an apparent undervalue, completed in under five years of the proposed mortgage you must be satisfied that the lender will be protected, if not arrange indemnity insurance.

You must obtain a clear bankruptcy search against all parties between a deed of gift or transaction that is an apparent under value.

POWERS OF ATTORNEY

Any document that is being executed under a Power of Attorney, you must ensure that the Power of Attorney is properly drawn, appears to be properly executed and the Attorney knows of no reason why such Power of Attorney will not be subsisting at completion.

Power of Attorney must not be used in connection with a regulated loan under the Consumer Credit Act 1974.

The original certified copy of the Power of Attorney must be sent with the deeds.

THE PROPERTY

Boundaries

These must be clearly defined by reference to a suitable plan or description.

Purchase price

This must be the same as set out in the instructions. Must advise the lender if there are any cash back or non-cash incentives.

Vacant possession

It is the term of the loan that Vacant possession is obtained unless otherwise stated.

New Properties

You must ensure that there is a National House Building Council Buildmark Scheme or similar.

Roads and Sewers

If not adopted, there must be a suitable agreement or a bond in existence.

Easements

All reasonable steps to check the property has the benefit of all easements.

Insurance

Where the lender does not arrange any insurance this must be arranged so that cover starts no later than completion.

Other occupiers

Rights of interested persons who are not a party to the mortgage who are or who will be in occupation of the premises may affect their right and you must obtain a signed deed or form of consent from all occupants age 17 or over.

Signing and Witnessing of Documents

Witnessing of documents is considered good practice so that the signature of a document that needs to be witnessed is witnessed by a solicitor, legal executive or licensed conveyancer.

All documents required at completion must be dated with the date of completion of the loan.

After completion you must register the mortgage with the HM Land Registry.

Your mortgage file.

For evidential purposes you must keep your file for at least six years from the date of the mortgage before destroying it.

Legal Costs

All charges and disbursements are payable by the buyer and should be collected on or before completion.

Non payment of fees or disbursements should not delay the stamping and registration of documents.

****

8

Completion and Post-Completion

Between exchange of contracts and completion –Preparing for Completion-Sellers checklist

- Check Transfer has been approved and requisitions replied to

- Received engrossed transfer from buyer – sign plan of the transfer.

- Seller to execute transfer in time for completion.

- Obtain mortgage redemption figure from mortgagees relating to all mortgages

- For leasehold obtain last receipts and make any apportionment necessary

- Prepare completion statement where necessary and send copies to buyer's solicitor in time for completion.

- Prepare an undertaking that needs to be given on completion for discharge of mortgage

- Locate title deeds and schedule to be handed over on completion

- Check arrangements for vacant possession and handing over keys

- Ensure estate agents are aware of completion arrangements

- Prepare bill and send to client

DOCUMENTS TO BE HANDED OVER ON COMPLETION

- Title deeds if unregistered, no land or charge certificate since October 2003, due to de-materialisation of deeds.

- END/ DS1 or undertaking

- Any money received for fixtures and fittings

- Arrange for keys to be released by agents

BETWEEN EXCHANGE OF CONTRACTS AND COMPLETION – PREPARING FOR COMPLETION – BUYERS CHECKLIST

- Transfer approved and requisitions satisfactorily answered

- Give power to execute mortgage deed

- Purchase deed and plan

- Send executed transfer to sellers solicitors in sufficient time for his client to sign prior to completion

- Do pre-completion searches – such as bankruptcy, OS1 for purchaser whole, OS2, purchaser part.

- Company search

- Make report on title to lender and request advance cheque in time for completion

- Received completion statement where necessary

- Remind client of arrangements for completion

- Check property insured

- Check arrangements for vacant possession and handing over of keys

- Ensure estate agents are aware on completion arrangements

- Make arrangements for transmission of completion money to sellers solicitors on the day of completion or where he has directed

AFTER COMPLETION – SELLERS CHECKLIST

- Confirm receipt of funds

- Telephone buyer's solicitors

- Telephone estate agent to confirm completion and authorise release of keys

- Inform client that completion has taken place

- Send Title Deeds and other relevant documents by first class post. DX on date of completion

- Transfer any purchase funds on related purchase

- Discharge existing mortgage by CHAPS or cheque with END or DS1 as required

- Pay estate agent's commission account

- Account to client for balance of proceeds of sale

- Transfer costs if agreed

- On receipt of DS1 or confirmation of END send or inform purchaser's solicitors and ask to be released from undertaking previously given to them.

- Remind client to cancel buildings insurance and notify public utilities

- Remind client of any Capital Gains Tax assessment which may be due

- Check file before placing in dead system

AFTER COMPLETION – BUYERS CHECKLIST

- Inform Client and Lender that completion has taken place

- Complete Mortgage Deed

- Complete file copies of Mortgage Deed and other relevant documents

- Arrange payment of Stamp Duty on the SDLT form. As this form now has to be signed by the purchaser's it would be wise to have this signed prior to completion at the same time as the transfer.

- If acting for a Company, register charge at Company's House within 21 days. This time limit is absolute and cannot be extended without an order of the court. Failing to register within the time limit will be an act of negligence by the solicitor.

- Pay off and deal with any undertakings concerning finance. Once SDLT form clear by the Revenue, and you are in receipt of the DS1 or END, register at Land Registry.

- On receipt of DS1 or confirmation of END, release seller's solicitors from their undertaking.

- Make application for Registration of Title within the relevant priority period.

- Serve a notice of assignment of Life policies or lease.

- On receipt of Title Information document from the Land Registry, check contents carefully.

- Deal with the custody of Deeds in accordance with the client's instructions or send to Lender to be held by them during the continuance of the Mortgage.

****

Glossary

A

Acting for both parties

There are limited circumstances when solicitors can act for both parties

Amount outstanding on the mortgage

Also known as the redemption figure

Apportionment of the purchase price

This may be used to save stamp duty land tax Fixtures and fittings known as chattels do not attract stamp duty and this is why the distinction between those and land is important.

Attorneys

A deed may be signed by an attorney but evidence of his power of attorney must be produced as this will be required by the land registry.

Auctions

The auction contract is usually prepared in advance. The purchaser has the right to undertake all his searches and enquiries and survey before the auction. Once the auction has been concluded usually a ten per cent deposit is taken and the sale takes place 28 days later. It would be necessary for anyone entering into an auction to have their finance in place before the hammer falls.

B

Boundaries

Even with a registered title the boundaries shown on the filed plan are general boundaries and are not definitive. The rule is generally what has been there for the last 12 years is the boundary this may have to be supported by statutory declarations.

Breach of a Restrictive Covenant

Or other defect. Indemnity insurance might be available

Bridging Finance

This might be for a deposit which is repaid on the sale of the property. It is rare for English banks to extend finance for a property that is open ended. It is usually only extended once contracts are exchange and there is a fixed date for completion.

Building Regulation Consent

This may be required even if there are not developments that require planning permission. It relates to health and safety matters and the type of materials used on completion of building works for which consent it required a final certificate must be obtained from the local authority. This is evidence that the building regulations have been complied with.

C

Capital Gains Tax

The main exemption which affects residential conveyancing is the principal private dwelling house exemption The seller must have occupied the dwelling house as his only or main residence throughout the period of ownership There is a sliding scale for absences and exemptions of short periods of absence

Capacity

The seller might be sole owner, joint owner, personal representative mortgagee, charity, company bankrupt or otherwise incapacitated.

Classes of Title

There are different classes of title the best being absolute title but there is also possessory title qualified title and good leasehold title

Contaminated Land

Any contamination could have serious effects in that it may be impossible to sell or obtain a mortgage on.

Completion

The day on which the transaction is finalised, the money changes hands and the parties vacate and take possession of the land that is the moving day.

Co-Ownership

This is where more than one person owns the land such as tenant in common or joint tenant.

Conveyancing

The process of transferring the ownership of freehold and leasehold land.

Compulsory Registration

This has arisen since 1990 and applies to the whole of England and Wales. The categories of events triggering a registration have changed but it is still not compulsory to register land without one of these triggers but voluntary registration could take place.

Conservation Area

Any non listed building in a conservation area must not be demolished with conservation area consent. There are also restrictions on development.

Contract Races

This is where more than one contract has been issued solicitors are obliged to let both parties know the terms of the race that is what needs to be done to secure the property. It must be confirmed in writing. A standard contact race would specific that the first person to be in a position to exchange contracts unconditionally wins the race. This is usually signified by the purchasers solicitors producing a signed contract and deposit cheque together with authority to proceed.

Covenants

This is a promise made in a deed and binding any subsequent owner of the land they may include such matter as maintaining the fences and only using the land for the erection of one property.

D

Deeds

Apart from unregistered land most deeds have now dematerialised as they are registered at the land registry. Evidence of ownership is shown by official copies of the registered entries. This is an official dated document showing the current state of the title.

Deposit

Although not a legal requirement is it customary and it's a form of security and part payment towards the purchase price.

Discharge of seller's mortgage

On completion is the seller has a mortgage this will need to be paid off and evidence given to the purchasers solicitor. This will need to be lodged at the land registry as proof of the discharge before a new purchaser can be substituted and maybe a new mortgage started.

Draft contract

The name attached to the contract before it is agreed by the parties and prior to exchange of contracts. Once the contract is approved it can be signed by the parties and forms the basis of the transactions. They must be in the same format. Identical contracts are exchanged.

E

Easements

This is a right over land of another such as a right of way or of light.

Engrossment

Merely means properly typed up version of a document the draft is amended then the engrossment is the fair copy

Escrow

A document such as contract mortgage transfer is delivered and will not become effective until some future date. It is therefore held in escrow the condition being that the event takes place such as completion or exchange of contracts. Gets rid of the need for all the parties to a transaction being in the same room at the same time.

Exchange of contracts

When the parties agree to bind themselves legally to buy and sell the land.

Execution

Means the signing of a document in a certain way for a deed to be valid it must contain the words this deed signed by the necessary parties in the presence of a witness and be delivered.

F

Filed plan

In conveyancing a plan is a map showing the land referred to edged in red. It is the official designation of the land for land registry purposes

Fixture and fittings

Now a formal part of the process in that purchasers solicitor will expect to see a completed fixtures and fittings form. It may be acceptable to apportion part of the price for fixtures and fittings and this is sometimes undertaken when the price falls on one of the bands for change in stamp duty. The list must be legitimate ad the revenue have the right to query this and levy any tax not paid

Fixtures and fittings distinction

Between objects not attached to the land are fittings and those attached are fixtures. The current fixtures and fitting list covers most eventualities but care should be taken if an offer is deemed to include items at the property they should be specifically mentioned in the contract.

Full Survey

As the name suggests this is full survey of the property and should contain a detailed breakdown of every aspect of the property.

H

Home Buyers Valuation and Survey Report

This is a compromise between a full structural survey and valuation.

I

Insurance

The risk on the property passes when contracts are exchanged. Even thought he purchaser has not got possession. The property is usually also insured by the seller up until the date of completion. They both have an insurable risk.

Indemnity Covenants

Any owner of land will remain liable for the covenants and passes these on by way of an indemnity covenant by any incoming purchaser

Investigating Title

Once the seller has produced the contract package the purchasers solicitors investigate title. This is to ensure that the seller is the owner of the property which is the subject of the contract. Also it must not reveal any defects other than those can be rectified prior to exchange of contracts.

There may for instance be consent required from a third party such as the necessity to register the transfer of a lease and become the member of a management company.

J

Joint tenants

This is most common between husband and wife. Both own equal shares in the property if either were to die the other inherit by way of survivorship. They cannot leave their share by will to anyone else.

L

Listed Building

Where a building might be of outstanding historic or architectural important the secretary of state may list it. Any alterations to the property will require both planning permission and listed building consent.

M

Mortgage

Is where the owner of land borrows money on the security of the land Also known as a legal charge. The lender has certain statutory powers the most important being that they can sell the property in the event of the loan not being paid.

Mortgage Fraud

Normally some proof of identity is required but this has been overtaken by the money laundering rules whereby it is accepted practice that clients should produce to their solicitors all the usual forms of ID to include utility bills driving licence passport etc.

Mortgages Repayments

The main types of repayment are pension, endowment and interest only. They do not affect the conveyancing transaction but some may have slightly different procedures between the conveyancers and the lender such as notices or deposit of insurance policies.

O

Occupiers Rights

The most important is the spouse of the seller. They have a statutory right to occupy the matrimonial home. Usually an enquiry is made as to there being any other occupiers of the matrimonial home. They are then asked to sign the contract to confirm they will give vacant possession completion.

Office Copy Entries

Usually refers to the registered title but can relate to any official copy issued by the land or other registries. They are acceptable as the originals.

Overriding Interests

These are matters affecting the land which are not on the register although this is being resolved under the current land registry rules. The most important being rights of way not mentioned on the deeds local land charges squatters rights.

P

Planning - Use of the property

It should be checked that the property has permission for its current use. Any purchaser should be aware that any change of use form its current use may require planning permission. For example a residential property may not be used for the fixing and selling of cars without a change of use. Any breach will be enforced by the local planning authority.

Planning Breach

This could be rectified by retrospective permission or again by indemnity insurance.

Purchase Deed

Now the transfer or TR1 this is the document that is signed by the seller transferring the land from the seller to the purchaser. It is signed prior to completion and once the formalities have been finalised such as the passing of the money it will be forwarded to the purchasers solicitors. This document will need to be stamped and registered at the land registry.

Possessory Title

The registry may grant a possessory title in the event of lack of paper title and eventually it can be upgraded to an absolute title. Land can be acquired through adverse possession but it is still subject to all covenants and easements etc existing at the date of the registration

Post Contract Stage

Between exchange of contracts and completion essential things such as finance is resolved as our final searches and all documents signed in readiness for completion.

R

Radon

If the property is in an area affected by radon gas a specific search should be undertaken which will reveal whether a survey has been undertaken and remedial measures have been taken.

Registered land

A state run system that proves the ownership of land by have a title registered at the HM land registry.

S

Searches

There are a series of searches. Before exchange of contracts the local authority search, after exchange bankruptcy and land registry searches.

Special Conditions

Any special condition will be used to vary the standard conditions of sale contained in the contract

Subject to Contract

This is of historical interest now as it is not possible to exchange contracts inadvertently or entering into irrevocably buying land without a proper contract. Some organisations still insist on using it as it gives them comfort Not now necessary in view of the Law Of Property (Miscellaneous) Provisions act 1989

Survey

There are many kinds of survey form the mere valuation by a lender to a full structural survey. Any purchaser should be aware that at the moment the law says *caveat emptor* that is let the buyer beware. Apart form a deliberate misstatement the seller is not liable for the current state of the property. An invariable practice is for purchasers to be advised to have a survey of the property and not to rely solely on the building society valuation.

Title

Either the registered or unregistered proof of the seller's ownership of the land.

Title Number

Every piece of registered land has a unique title number and must be used in all official documents searches etc.

Tenants in Common

Is where two or more people own land jointly in separate shares. Either owner can pass their share by will to anyone they wish.

Tenure

The legal term for how the land is being held being either freehold or leasehold.

U

Unregistered Land

The seller has to prove title by a series of documents such as conveyances, mortgagees etc now being replaced by registered conveyancing.

Undertakings

These are promises by solicitor to undertake certain acts. The most common being that the sellers solicitor will discharge the existing mortgage. Failure to comply with the undertaking is a professional offence so therefore they will not be entered into lightly and can be relied up They should always be confirmed in writing and their terms made certain.

Upgrading Title

Either on application or on the initiative of the registrar a title may be upgraded such as possessory to absolute and the same for qualified and good leasehold title

V

Valuation

Can either be an estate agents valuation which is a financial matter for the purchasers and sellers a lenders valuation is the figure that is used to calculate how much the lender is prepared to lend. This is based on a valuers report prepared for the lender once the buyer has requested a loan. It is an assessment of the value not a survey of the property. Lenders will normally exclude liability for any defects in the property. They are not undertaking that the property is fit for its purpose just because they are prepared to lend on it.

Value Added Tax – VAT

Is payable on solicitors costs but not o the purchase price of second hand properties. There is not VAT payable on stamp duty or land registry fees in a domestic transaction.

W

Witnesses

Must be a responsible adult and is usually independent of the parties who must add name, address and occupation

SALE 0F PROPERTY

STANDARD LETTERS

Letter to Building Society / Bank Requesting Title Deeds

21 November, 2015

Address

Dear Sirs

Re   Property:
Account Number:
Borrower:

We act for the above named clients in connection with the sale of the above property and we shall be obliged if you would please send us have the Title Deeds relating to this property.

We undertake to hold them to your order pending redemption of the mortgage.

At the same time please let us know the amount owing under this mortgage.

Yours faithfully

Letter to Estate Agent Acknowledging Sales Particulars

21 November, 2015

Address

Dear Sirs

Re   Property:
**   Our Client:**

We acknowledge safe receipt of your sales particulars and we confirm we have today contacted the purchaser's solicitors with a view to issuing a draft Contract.

Yours faithfully

Authority to Bank to Obtain Title Deeds

21 November, 2015

Address

Dear Sirs

We hereby give you authority to release the Title Deeds for property listed below to …………….. of …………….

Address of Property: ………………………………………

Address of Lender: ………………………………………

Account Number: ………………………………………

Signature ………………………………………

Signature ………………………………………

First Letter to Purchaser's Solicitors

21 November, 2015

Address

Dear Sirs

Re **Property:**
  Your Client:
  Our Client:

We understand that you act on behalf of ??????? of ?????????????? in connection with their proposed purchase of the above from our clients ?????????????.

We would be obliged if you could confirm that if your clients have a property to sell a purchaser has been found and if your client should require finance this has been approved at least in principle.

Subject to the above being confirmed we will arrange for a draft Contract to be issued to you as soon as possible.

Yours faithfully

Letter Issuing Contract etc to Purchaser's Solicitors

21 November, 2015

Address

Dear Sirs

Re   Property:
      Your Client:
      Our Client:

Thank you for your letter of ????????. We take this opportunity of enclosing:

1. Draft Contract in duplicate

2. Official Copy of Register Entries plus File Plan

3. Fixtures Fittings and Contents List

4. Seller's Property Information Form

5. Copy Transfer dated ???????????

Yours faithfully

Letter to Purchaser' Solicitor on Completion

21 November, 2015

Fax & Post

Fax Number: ....

Address

Dear Sirs

Re   Property:
Your Client:
Our Client:

We acknowledge safe receipt of your Telegraphic Transfer in the sum of £........ and we take this opportunity of enclosing the following:

1. TR1

2. Land Certificate number ....

3. All Pre-registration documents

Kindly acknowledge safe receipt.

We confirm that we have today telephoned the agents to release the keys.

Yours faithfully

Letter Sending Approved TR1 and Replies to Requisitions on Title

21 November, 2015

Address

Dear Sirs

Re   Property:
      Your Client:
      Our Client:

Thank you for your letter of ………… we take this opportunity of enclosing the following:

1. TR1 approved as amended

2. Requisitions on Title and our replies thereto

Yours faithfully

Letter to Purchaser's Solicitor on Exchange of Contracts

21 November, 2015
Fax & Post
Fax Number:

Address

Dear Sirs

Re   **Property:**
        Your Client:
        Our Client:

Further to our telephone conversation at 2:15 p.m. between ......
and .... Contracts were exchanged and the date fixed
for completion is ....

The sale price is £....... and you will be holding the £........
deposit strictly to our order pending completion.

We enclose our client's part of the Contract to complete
exchange of Contracts. .

Yours faithfully

Letter to Estate Agents requesting Commission Account

21 November, 2015

Address

Dear Sirs

**Re   Property:
         Client:**

We write to confirm Contracts have now been exchanged in this matter. The date fixed for completion being the ....

We await hearing from you with your commission account.

Yours faithfully

Letter to Bank/Building Society Requesting Redemption Figure

21 November, 2015

Building Society
Address

Dear Sirs

Re: Borrower:
Property:
Account No:

Would you please let us have the redemption figure on the above mortgage account as at *date*.......

Yours faithfully

Letter Informing Utilities of Sale

21 November, 2015

Address

Dear Sirs

Re   Owner:
        Property:
        Account No:

We take this opportunity of advising you that the above property has now been sold and as from .... the new occupants will be ....

Yours faithfully

PURCHASE PROPERTY

STANDARD LETTERS

First Letter to Seller's Solicitors

21 November, 2015

Address

For the attention of:

Dear Sirs

Re   **Property:**
               Our Client:
               Your Client:

We act on behalf of .... and .... our clients finance is approved in principle and we await hearing from you with draft paperwork.

Yours faithfully

Letter to Seller's Solicitor Returning Draft Contract Approved

21 November, 2015

Address

For the attention of:

Dear Sirs

Re   **Property:**
                              Our Client:
                              Your Client:

Thank you for your letter of .... we take this opportunity of enclosing the draft Contract duly approved.

We will use the top copy as the engrossment.

Yours faithfully

Letter to Seller's Solicitor on Exchange of Contracts

21 November, 2015
Fax & Post
Fax Number:

Address

Dear Sirs

Re   Property:
Your Client:
Our Client:

Further to our telephone conversation at 2:15 p.m. between ......
and .... Contracts were exchanged and the date fixed
for completion is ....

The purchase price is £....... and we will be holding the £........
deposit strictly to your order pending completion.

We enclose our client's part of the Contract to complete
exchange of Contracts. .

Yours faithfully

Letter to Seller's Solicitors Sending TR1 with Requisitions on Title

21 November, 2015

Address

Dear Sirs

Re   Property:
**   Your Client:**
**   Our Client:**

Thank you for your letter of ………… we take this opportunity of enclosing the following:

1. TR1 in duplicate

2. Requisitions on Title

Yours faithfully

Letter to Seller's Solicitor Confirming Purchase Money Sent

21 November, 2015
Fax & Post
Fax Number:

Address

Dear Sirs

Re   Property:
Your Client:
Our Client:

We are writing to confirm we have today telegraphically transferred to you the sum of £……….. being the balance required to complete this matter.

We await hearing from you with a dated and executed Transfer and all the other Title Deeds relating to the property.

We would be obliged if on receipt of the money you could kindly telephone the agents to release the keys.

Yours faithfully

SCHEDULE OF DOCUMENTS TO BE USED IN CONVEYANCING

1) PROTOCOL FORMS (see overleaf)

    a) Fixtures, Fittings and Contents (4th Edition)

    b) Sellers Property Information Form (4th Edition)

    c) Sellers Leasehold Information Form (3rd Edition)

2) General Leasehold Enquiries (see overleaf)

3) Land Registry Forms

    a) SIM

    b) OC1

    c) D1

    d) TR1

    e) TP1

    f) OS1

    g) OS2

    h) DS1

    i) FR1

    j) AP1

4) Various Search Forms

    a) Local Authority Search LLC1

    b) Standard Enquiries for Local Authority (2002 edition)

5)   Stamp Duty Land Tax – Land transaction return (SDLT1) and Self Certificate SDLT60

6)   Completion Information and Requisitions on Title

7)   Draft contract

****

Fittings and Contents Form (2nd edition)

Address of the property

Postcode ☐☐☐☐☐☐☐

Full names of the seller

Seller's solicitor

Name of solicitors firm

Address

Email

Reference number

Definitions

- 'Seller' means all sellers together where the property is owned by more than one person

- 'Buyer' means all buyers together where the property is being bought by more than one person

The Law Society

www.lawsociety.org.uk

Laserform International 12/10

Instructions to the seller and the buyer

This form must be completed accurately by the seller. It may become part of the contract between the seller and the buyer.

The seller should make a clear statement of what is included in the sale of the property by marking each box in this form with a ✓ or a **X**, as shown below:

Included in the sale of the property	✓
Not included in the sale of the property	**X**

The seller may be prepared to sell to the buyer an item which is otherwise not included in the sale of the property. In this case, the seller should mark the appropriate box with a **X** to show the item is not included, followed by the amount that the seller wishes to be paid for the item, as shown below.

Not included, but for sale at an extra cost	**X**{amount}

The buyer can then decide whether to accept the seller's offer. The seller and buyer should inform their solicitors of any arrangements made about items offered for sale in this way.

If the seller removes any fixtures and fittings, the seller must make good any damage caused by their removal.

If the seller removes a light fitting, it is assumed that the seller will replace the fitting with a ceiling rose and socket, a flex, bulb holder and bulb.

The seller is responsible for removing any possessions, including rubbish, from the property, the garage, the garden and any outbuildings or sheds.

The seller and the buyer should check the information given on the form carefully.

1 Basic fittings

Boiler / immersion heater		Roof insulation	
Radiators / wall heaters		Window fitments	
Night-storage heaters		Window shutters / grills	
Free-standing heaters		Internal door furniture	
Gas fires (with surround)		External door furniture	
Electric fires (with surround)		Doorbell / chime	
Light switches		Electric sockets	

2 Television and telephone

Telephone receivers		Television aerial	
Radio aerial		Satellite dish	

3 Kitchen

Hob		Refrigerator / fridge-freezer	
Extractor hood		Freezer	
Fitted oven and grills		Free-standing oven / cooker	
Fitted microwave		Dishwasher	
Tumble-dryer		Washing machine	

4 Bathroom

Bath		Separate shower and fittings	
Shower fitting for bath		Towel rail	
Shower curtain		Soap / toothbrush holders	
Bathroom cabinet		Toilet roll holders	
Taps		Bathroom mirror	

5 Carpets, curtains, light fittings and fitted units

	Carpets	Curtain rails poles/pelmets*	Curtains/ blinds*	Light fittings	Fitted units**
Hall, stairs and landing					
Living room					
Dining room					
Kitchen					
Bedroom 1					
Bedroom 2					
Bedroom 3					

If the seller wishes to further explain the answers to section 5 above, please give details:

* Delete as appropriate.
** Fitted units (for example: fitted cupboards, fitted shelves, and fitted wardrobes).

6 Outdoor area

Garden furniture		Outdoor heater	
Garden ornaments		Stock of fuel	
Trees, plants, shrubs		Outside lights	
Barbecue		Water butt	
Dustbins		Clothes line	
Garden shed		Rotary line	
Greenhouse			

Signed: .... Dated: ....

Each seller should sign this form.

Law Society Property Information Form (3rd edition)

Address of the property

Postcode ☐☐☐☐☐☐☐☐

Full names of the seller

Seller's solicitor

Name of solicitor's firm

Address

Email

Reference number

About this form

This form is completed by the seller to supply the detailed information and documents which may be relied upon for the conveyancing process.

It is important that sellers and buyers read the notes below.

Definitions

- 'Seller' means all sellers together where the property is owned by more than one person.
- 'Buyer' means all buyers together where the property is being bought by more than one person.
- 'Property' includes all buildings and land within its boundaries.

The Law Society

www.lawsociety.org.uk

Instructions to the seller

- The answers should be prepared by the person or persons who are named as owner on the deeds or Land Registry title or by the owner's legal representative(s) if selling under a power of attorney or grant of probate or representation. If there is more than one seller, you should prepare the answers together or, if only one seller prepares the form, the other(s) should check the answers given and all sellers should sign the form.

- If you do not know the answer to any question, you must say so. If you are unsure of the meaning of any questions or answers, please ask your solicitor. Completing this form is not mandatory, but omissions or delay in providing some information may delay the sale.

- If you later become aware of any information which would alter any replies you have given, you must inform your solicitor immediately. This is as important as giving the right answers in the first place. Do not change any arrangements concerning the property with anyone (such as a tenant or neighbour) without first consulting your solicitor.

- It is very important that your answers are accurate. If you give incorrect or incomplete information to the buyer (on this form or otherwise in writing or in conversation, whether through your estate agent or solicitor or directly to the buyer), the buyer may make a claim for compensation from you or refuse to complete the purchase.

- You should answer the questions based upon information known to you (or, in the case of legal representatives, you or the owner). You are not expected to have expert knowledge of legal or technical matters, or matters that occurred prior to your ownership of the property.

- Please give your solicitor any letters, agreements or other papers which help answer the questions. If you are aware of any which you are not supplying with the answers, tell your solicitor. If you do not have any documentation you may need to obtain copies at your own expense. Also pass to your solicitor any notices you have received concerning the property and any which arrive at any time before completion of the sale.

Instructions to the buyer

- If the seller gives you, separately from this form, any information concerning the property (in writing or in conversation, whether through an estate agent or solicitor or directly to you) on which you wish to rely when buying the property, you should tell your solicitor.

- You are entitled to rely on the replies given to enquiries but in relation to the physical condition of the property, the replies should not be treated as a substitute for undertaking your own survey or making your own independent enquiries, which you are recommended to do.

- The seller is only obliged to give answers based on their own information. They may not have knowledge of legal or technical matters. You should not expect the seller to have knowledge of, or give information about, matters prior to their ownership of the property.

If the property is leasehold this section, or parts of it, may not apply.

1.1 Looking towards the property from the road, who owns or accepts responsibility to maintain or repair the boundary features:

(a) on the left?

- [ ] Seller
- [ ] Shared
- [ ] Neighbour
- [ ] Not known

(b) on the right?

- [ ] Seller
- [ ] Shared
- [ ] Neighbour
- [ ] Not known

(c) at the rear?

- [ ] Seller
- [ ] Shared
- [ ] Neighbour
- [ ] Not known

(d) at the front?

- [ ] Seller
- [ ] Shared
- [ ] Neighbour
- [ ] Not known

1.2 If the boundaries are irregular please indicate ownership by written description or by reference to a plan:

1.3 Is the seller aware of any boundary feature having been moved in the last 20 years? If Yes, please give details:

- [ ] Yes
- [ ] No

1.4 During the seller's ownership, has any land previously forming part of the property been sold or has any adjacent property been purchased? If Yes, please give details:

- [ ] Yes
- [ ] No

1.5 Does any part of the property or any building on the property overhang, or project under, the boundary of the neighbouring property or road? If Yes, please give details:

- [ ] Yes
- [ ] No

1 Boundaries (continued)

1.6 Has any notice been received under the Party Wall Act 1996 in respect of any shared/party boundaries? If Yes, please supply a copy, and give details of any works carried out or agreed:

☐ Yes ☐ No
☐ Enclosed ☐ To follow

2 Disputes and complaints

2.1 Have there been any disputes or complaints regarding this property or a property nearby? If Yes, please give details:

☐ Yes ☐ No

2.2 Is the seller aware of anything which might lead to a dispute about the property or a property nearby? If Yes, please give details:

☐ Yes ☐ No

3 Notices and proposals

3.1 Have any notices or correspondence been received or sent (e.g. from or to a neighbour, council or government department), or any negotiations or discussions taken place, which affect the property or a property nearby? If Yes, please give details:

☐ Yes ☐ No

3.2 Is the seller aware of any proposals to develop property or land nearby, or of any proposals to make alterations to buildings nearby? If Yes, please give details:

☐ Yes ☐ No

Note to seller: All relevant approvals and supporting paperwork referred to in section 4 of this form, such as listed building consents, planning permissions, Building Regulations consents and completion certificates should be provided. If the seller has had works carried out the seller should produce the documentation authorising this. Copies may be obtained from the relevant local authority website. Competent Persons Certificates may be obtained from the contractor or the scheme provider (e.g. FENSA or Gas Safe Register). Further information about Competent Persons Certificates can be found at: **www.gov.uk**.

Note to buyer: If any alterations or improvements have been made since the property was last valued for council tax, the sale of the property may trigger a revaluation. This may mean that following completion of the sale, the property will be put into a higher council tax band. Further information about council tax valuation can be found at: **www.voa.gov.uk**.

4.1 Have any of the following changes been made to the whole or any part of the property (including the garden)?

(a) Building works (e.g. extension, loft or garage conversion, removal of internal walls). If Yes, please give details including dates of all work undertaken:

☐ Yes ☐ No

(b) Change of use (e.g. from an office to a residence)

☐ Yes ☐ No
[ ] Year

(c) Installation of replacement windows, roof windows, roof lights, glazed doors since 1 April 2002

☐ Yes ☐ No
[ ] Year(s)

(d) Addition of a conservatory

☐ Yes ☐ No
[ ] Year

4.2 If Yes to any of the questions in 4.1 and if the work was undertaken during the seller's ownership of the property:

(a) please supply copies of the planning permissions, Building Regulations approvals and Completion Certificates, OR:

(b) if none were required, please explain why these were not required – e.g. permitted development rights applied or the work was exempt from Building Regulations:

Further information about permitted development can be found at: **www.planningportal.gov.uk**.

4.3 Are any of the works disclosed in 4.1 above unfinished?
If Yes, please give details:

☐ Yes ☐ No

4.4 Is the seller aware of any breaches of planning permission conditions or Building Regulations consent conditions, unfinished work or work that does not have all necessary consents? If Yes, please give details:

☐ Yes ☐ No

4.5 Are there any planning or building control issues to resolve?
If Yes, please give details:

☐ Yes ☐ No

4.6 Have solar panels been installed?

☐ Yes ☐ No

If Yes:

(a) In what year were the solar panels installed?

☐ Year

(b) Are the solar panels owned outright?

☐ Yes ☐ No

(c) Has a long lease of the roof/air space been granted to a solar panel provider? If Yes, please supply copies of the relevant documents.

☐ Yes ☐ No
☐ Enclosed ☐ To follow

4.7 Is the property or any part of it:

(a) a listed building?

☐ Yes ☐ No
☐ Not known

(b) in a conservation area?

☐ Yes ☐ No
☐ Not known

If Yes, please supply copies of any relevant documents.

☐ Enclosed ☐ To follow

4.8 Are any of the trees on the property subject to a
Tree Preservation Order?

☐ Yes ☐ No
☐ Not known

If Yes:

(a) Have the terms of the Order been complied with?

☐ Yes ☐ No
☐ Not known

(b) Please supply a copy of any relevant documents.

☐ Enclosed ☐ To follow

5 Guarantees and warranties

Note to seller: All available guarantees, warranties and supporting paperwork should be supplied before exchange of contracts.

Note to buyer: Some guarantees only operate to protect the person who had the work carried out or may not be valid if their terms have been breached. You may wish to contact the company to establish whether it is still trading and if so, whether the terms of the guarantee will apply to you.

5.1 Does the property benefit from any of the following guarantees or warranties? If Yes, please supply a copy.

(a) New home warranty (e.g. NHBC or similar)

☐ Yes ☐ No
☐ Enclosed ☐ To follow

(b) Damp proofing

☐ Yes ☐ No
☐ Enclosed ☐ To follow

(c) Timber treatment

☐ Yes ☐ No
☐ Enclosed ☐ To follow

(d) Windows, roof lights, roof windows or glazed doors

☐ Yes ☐ No
☐ Enclosed ☐ To follow

(e) Electrical work

☐ Yes ☐ No
☐ Enclosed ☐ To follow

(f) Roofing

☐ Yes ☐ No
☐ Enclosed ☐ To follow

(g) Central heating

☐ Yes ☐ No
☐ Enclosed ☐ To follow

(h) Underpinning

☐ Yes ☐ No
☐ Enclosed ☐ To follow

(i) Other (please state):

☐ Enclosed ☐ To follow

5.2 Have any claims been made under any of these guarantees or warranties? If Yes, please give details:

☐ Yes ☐ No

6 Insurance

6.1 Does the seller insure the property?

☐ Yes ☐ No

6.2 Has any buildings insurance taken out by the seller ever been:

(a) subject to an abnormal rise in premiums?

☐ Yes ☐ No

(b) subject to high excesses?

☐ Yes ☐ No

(c) subject to unusual conditions?

☐ Yes ☐ No

(d) refused?

☐ Yes ☐ No

If Yes, please give details:

6.3 Has the seller made any buildings insurance claims? If Yes, please give details:

☐ Yes ☐ No

Flooding

Note: Flooding may take a variety of forms: it may be seasonal or irregular or simply a one-off occurrence. The property does not need to be near a sea or river for flooding to occur. Further information about flooding can be found at: **www.defra.gov.uk**.

7.1 Has any part of the property (whether buildings or surrounding garden or land) ever been flooded? If Yes, please state when the flooding occurred and identify the parts that flooded:

☐ Yes   ☐ No

If No to question 7.1 please continue to 7.3 and do not answer 7.2 below.

7.2 What type of flooding occurred?

(a)	Ground water	☐ Yes	☐ No
(b)	Sewer flooding	☐ Yes	☐ No
(c)	Surface water	☐ Yes	☐ No
(d)	Coastal flooding	☐ Yes	☐ No
(e)	River flooding	☐ Yes	☐ No

(f) Other (please state):

7.3 Has a Flood Risk Report been prepared? If Yes, please supply a copy.

☐ Yes   ☐ No
☐ Enclosed   ☐ To follow

Further information about the types of flooding and Flood Risk Reports can be found at: **www.environment-agency.gov.uk**.

Radon

Note: Radon is a naturally occurring inert radioactive gas found in the ground. Some parts of England and Wales are more adversely affected by it than others. Remedial action is advised for properties with a test result above the 'recommended action level'. Further information about Radon can be found at: **www.hpa.org.uk**.

7.4 Has a Radon test been carried out on the property?

☐ Yes   ☐ No

If Yes:

(a) please supply a copy of the report

☐ Enclosed   ☐ To follow

(b) was the test result below the 'recommended action level'?

☐ Yes   ☐ No

7.5 Were any remedial measures undertaken on construction to reduce Radon gas levels in the property?

☐ Yes   ☐ No
☐ Not known

Energy efficiency

Note: An Energy Performance Certificate (EPC) is a document that gives information about a property's energy usage. Further information about EPCs can be found at: **www.gov.uk**.

7.6 Please supply a copy of the EPC for the property.

☐ Enclosed   ☐ To follow
☐ Already supplied

7.7 Have any installations in the property been financed under the Green Deal scheme? If Yes, please give details of all installations and supply a copy of your last electricity bill.

☐ Yes   ☐ No
☐ Enclosed   ☐ To follow

Further information about the Green Deal can be found at: **www.gov.uk/decc**.

Japanese knotweed

Note: Japanese knotweed is an invasive plant that can cause damage to property. It can take several years to eradicate.

7.8 Is the property affected by Japanese knotweed?

☐ Yes   ☐ No
☐ Not known

If Yes, please state whether there is a Japanese knotweed management plan in place and supply a copy.

☐ Yes   ☐ No
☐ Not known
☐ Enclosed   ☐ To follow

8 Rights and informal arrangements

Note: Rights and arrangements may relate to access or shared use. They may also include leases of less than seven years, rights to mines and minerals, manorial rights, chancel repair and similar matters. If you are uncertain about whether a right or arrangement is covered by this question, please ask your solicitor.

8.1 Does ownership of the property carry a responsibility to contribute towards the cost of any jointly used services, such as maintenance of a private road, a shared driveway, a boundary or drain? If Yes, please give details:

☐ Yes   ☐ No

8.2 Does the property benefit from any rights or arrangements over any neighbouring property? If Yes, please give details: ☐ Yes   ☐ No

8.3 Has anyone taken steps to prevent access to the property, or to complain about or demand payment for access to the property? If Yes, please give details: ☐ Yes   ☐ No

8.4 Does the seller know of any of the following rights or arrangements which affect the property?

(a)	Rights of light	☐ Yes ☐ No
(b)	Rights of support from adjoining properties	☐ Yes ☐ No
(c)	Customary rights (e.g. rights deriving from local traditions)	☐ Yes ☐ No
(d)	Other people's rights to mines and minerals under the land	☐ Yes ☐ No
(e)	Chancel repair liability	☐ Yes ☐ No
(f)	Other people's rights to take things from the land (such as timber, hay or fish)	☐ Yes ☐ No

If Yes, please give details:

8.5 Are there any other rights or arrangements affecting the property? If Yes, please give details: ☐ Yes   ☐ No

Services crossing the property or neighbouring property

8.6 Do any drains, pipes or wires serving the property cross any neighbour's property?   ☐ Yes   ☐ No   ☐ Not known

8.7 Do any drains, pipes or wires leading to any neighbour's property cross the property?   ☐ Yes   ☐ No   ☐ Not known

8.8 Is there any agreement or arrangement about drains, pipes or wires?

☐ Yes   ☐ No
☐ Not known

If Yes, please supply a copy or give details:

☐ Enclosed   ☐ To follow

9 Parking

9.1 What are the parking arrangements at the property?

9.2 Is the property in a controlled parking zone or within a local authority parking scheme?

☐ Yes   ☐ No
☐ Not known

10 Other charges

Note: If the property is leasehold, details of lease expenses such as service charges and ground rent should be set out on the separate TA7 Leasehold Information Form. If the property is freehold, there may still be charges: for example, payments to a management company or for the use of a private drainage system.

10.1 Does the seller have to pay any charges relating to the property (excluding any payments such as council tax, utility charges, etc.), for example payments to a management company? If Yes, please give details:

☐ Yes   ☐ No

11 Occupiers

11.1 Does the seller live at the property?

☐ Yes   ☐ No

11.2 Does anyone else, aged 17 or over, live at the property?

☐ Yes   ☐ No

If No to question 11.2, please continue to section 12 'Services' and do not answer 11.3–11.5 below.

11.3 Please give the full names of any occupiers (other than the sellers) aged 17 or over:

11.4 Are any of the occupiers (other than the sellers), aged 17 or over, tenants or lodgers?   ☐ Yes   ☐ No

11.5 Is the property being sold with vacant possession?   ☐ Yes   ☐ No

If Yes, have all the occupiers aged 17 or over:

(a) agreed to leave prior to completion?   ☐ Yes   ☐ No

(b) agreed to sign the sale contract? If No, please supply other evidence that the property will be vacant on completion.   ☐ Yes   ☐ No   ☐ Enclosed   ☐ To follow

12 Services

Note: If the seller does not have a certificate requested below this can be obtained from the relevant Competent Persons Scheme. Further information about Competent Persons Schemes can be found at: **www.gov.uk**.

Electricity

12.1 Has the whole or any part of the electrical installation been tested by a qualified and registered electrician?   ☐ Yes   ☐ No

If Yes, please state the year it was tested and provide a copy of the test certificate.   ☐ Year   ☐ Enclosed   ☐ To follow

12.2 Has the property been rewired or had any electrical installation work carried out since 1 January 2005?   ☐ Yes   ☐ No   ☐ Not known

If Yes, please supply one of the following:

(a) a copy of the signed BS7671 Electrical Safety Certificate   ☐ Enclosed   ☐ To follow

(b) the installer's Building Regulations Compliance Certificate   ☐ Enclosed   ☐ To follow

(c) the Building Control Completion Certificate   ☐ Enclosed   ☐ To follow

Central heating

12.3 Does the property have a central heating system?   ☐ Yes   ☐ No

If Yes:

(a) What type of system is it (e.g. mains gas, liquid gas, oil, electricity, etc.)?

(b) When was the heating system installed? If on or after 1 April 2005 please supply a copy of the 'completion certificate' (e.g. CORGI or Gas Safe Register) or the 'exceptional circumstances' form.   ☐ Date

☐ Not known
☐ Enclosed   ☐ To follow

(c) Is the heating system in good working order?   ☐ Yes   ☐ No

(d) In what year was the heating system last serviced/maintained? Please supply a copy of the inspection report.   ☐ Year ☐ Not known
☐ Enclosed   ☐ To follow
☐ Not available

Drainage and sewerage

Note: Further information about drainage and sewerage can be found at: **www.environment-agency.gov.uk**.

12.4 Is the property connected to mains:

(a) foul water drainage?   ☐ Yes   ☐ No
☐ Not known

(b) surface water drainage?   ☐ Yes   ☐ No
☐ Not known

If Yes to both questions in 12.4, please continue to section 13 'Connection to utilities and services' and do not answer 12.5–12.10 below.

12.5 Is sewerage for the property provided by:

(a) a septic tank?   ☐ Yes   ☐ No

(b) a sewage treatment plant?   ☐ Yes   ☐ No

(c) cesspool?   ☐ Yes   ☐ No

12.6 Is the use of the septic tank, sewage treatment plant or cesspool shared with other properties? If Yes, how many properties share the system?   ☐ Yes   ☐ No
☐ Properties share

12.7 When was the system last emptied?
[ ] Year

12.8 If the property is served by a sewage treatment plant, when was the treatment plant last serviced?
[ ] Year

12.9 When was the system installed?
[ ] Year

Note: Some systems installed after 1 January 1991 require Building Regulations approval, environmental permits or registration. Further information about permits and registration can be found at: **www.environment-agency.gov.uk**.

12.10 Is any part of the septic tank, sewage treatment plant (including any soakaway or outfall) or cesspool, or the access to it, outside the boundary of the property? If Yes, please supply a plan showing the location of the system and how access is obtained.

[ ] Yes [ ] No
[ ] Enclosed [ ] To follow

---

13 Connection to utilities and services

Please mark the Yes or No boxes to show which of the following utilities and services are connected to the property and give details of any providers.

Mains electricity Yes [ ] No [ ]

Provider's name

Location of meter

Mains gas Yes [ ] No [ ]

Provider's name

Location of meter

Mains water Yes [ ] No [ ]

Provider's name

Location of stopcock

Location of meter, if any

Mains sewerage Yes [ ] No [ ]

Provider's name

Telephone Yes [ ] No [ ]

Provider's name

Cable Yes [ ] No [ ]

Provider's name

14.1 Is this sale dependent on the seller completing the purchase of another property on the same day?

☐ Yes   ☐ No

14.2 Does the seller have any special requirements about a moving date? If Yes, please give details:

☐ Yes   ☐ No

14.3 Does the sale price exceed the amount necessary to repay all mortgages and charges secured on the property?

☐ Yes   ☐ No

14.4 Will the seller ensure that:

(a) all rubbish is removed from the property (including from the loft, garden, outbuildings, garages and sheds) and that the property will be left in a clean and tidy condition?

☐ Yes   ☐ No

(b) if light fittings are removed, the fittings will be replaced with ceiling rose, flex, bulb holder and bulb?

☐ Yes   ☐ No

(c) reasonable care will be taken when removing any other fittings or contents?

☐ Yes   ☐ No

(d) keys to all windows and doors and details of alarm codes will be left at the property or with the estate agent?

☐ Yes   ☐ No

Signed: ....   Dated: ....

Signed: ....   Dated: ....

Each seller should sign this form.

The Law Society is the representative body for solicitors in England and Wales.

Leasehold information form

Document date [ ] / [ ] / [ ]

Address of the property

Postcode [ ][ ][ ][ ][ ][ ][ ]

This form should be completed and read in conjunction with the explanatory notes available separately

1 Other leases

1.1 Is there any headlease?

If Yes, please supply a copy.

☐ Yes ☐ No ☐ Enclosed
☐ To follow ☐ Not known

1.2 Is there any underlease?

If Yes, please supply a copy.

☐ Yes ☐ No ☐ Enclosed
☐ To follow ☐ Not known

1.3 In respect of any headlease or underlease of the whole or any part of the property, state any amounts owing or owed by or to the seller relating to rent, service charge, insurance premiums or other financial contribution.

The Law Society

www.hips.lawsociety.org.uk

TA7
© Law Society 2007

Laserform International 8/07

2 Management company

2.1 Is there a management company which is run by the tenants? ☐ Yes ☐ No

If Yes, please supply copies of the following:

(a) Memorandum and articles of association ☐ Enclosed ☐ To follow

(b) The share or membership certificate ☐ Enclosed ☐ To follow

(c) The company's accounts for the last three years ☐ Enclosed ☐ To follow

(d) The names and addresses of the secretary and treasurer of the company:

2.2 Has the management company been dissolved or removed from the register at Companies House? ☐ Yes ☐ No

3 Maintenance charges

3.1 Have there been any problems in the last three years between flat owners and the landlord or management company about maintenance charges, or the method of management? ☐ Yes ☐ No

If Yes, please give details:

3.2 Has there been any challenge to the maintenance charges or any expense in the last three years? ☐ Yes ☐ No

If Yes, please give details:

3.3 Has the landlord had any problems with collecting the maintenance charges from other flat owners? □ Yes □ No

If Yes, please give details:

---

4 Notices and consents

4.1 Has a notice been received from any landlord or landlord's agent? □ Yes □ No □ Enclosed □ To follow

If Yes, please supply a copy.

4.2 Has any other notice been received from any other person or authority? □ Yes □ No □ Enclosed □ To follow

If Yes, please supply a copy.

4.3 Are any changes to the terms of the lease proposed or has the landlord given any consents under the lease? (This could be in a formal document, a letter or even oral). □ Yes □ No □ Enclosed □ To follow

If Yes, please give details or supply a copy.

4.4 Please provide the name and address of the landlord or landlord's agent for service of any notice of change of ownership. □ To follow □ Not applicable

Note: A notice could be on a printed form or in the form of a letter and a buyer will wish to know if anything of this sort has been received.

Leasehold information form **TA7**

5 Complaints

5.1 Has the seller received any complaint from the landlord, any other landlord, management company or any other occupier about anything the seller has or has not done?

☐ Yes   ☐ No

If Yes, please give details:

5.2 Has the seller complained or does the seller have cause for complaint to or about the landlord, management company or any other occupier?

☐ Yes   ☐ No

If Yes, please give details:

6 Buildings insurance of the property

6.1 Is the seller responsible under the terms of the lease for arranging the buildings insurance of the property?

☐ Yes   ☐ No

If Yes, please supply copies of:

(a) the insurance policy   ☐ Enclosed   ☐ To follow

(b) the receipt for the last payment of the premium   ☐ Enclosed   ☐ To follow

6.2 Is the landlord or management company responsible for arranging the buildings insurance of the property?

☐ Yes   ☐ No

If Yes, please supply copies of:

(a) the insurance policy   ☐ Enclosed   ☐ To follow

(b) the schedule for the current year   ☐ Enclosed   ☐ To follow

6.3 Do the insurers record the interests of the buyer's mortgagee and the buyer on the policy?

☐ Yes   ☐ No   ☐ Not known

7 Decoration

7.1 When was the outside of the building last decorated?

In the year [ ]   ☐ Not known

7.2 When were any internal communal parts last decorated?

In the year [ ]   ☐ Not known

7.3 When was the inside of the property last decorated?

In the year [ ]   ☐ Not known

8 Alterations

8.1 Is the seller aware of any alterations having been made to the property since the lease was originally granted?

☐ Yes   ☐ No   ☐ Not known

If Yes, please give details:

[ ]

8.2 If alterations have been made to the property since the lease was originally granted, was the landlord's consent obtained?

If Yes, please supply copies of any consents obtained.

☐ Yes   ☐ No
☐ Enclosed   ☐ To follow
☐ Not known   ☐ Not required

9 Occupation

9.1 Is the seller now occupying the property as their sole or main home?

☐ Yes   ☐ No

9.2 Has the seller occupied the property as their sole or main home (apart from usual holidays and business trips):

(a) continuously throughout the last 12 months?

☐ Yes   ☐ No

(b) continuously throughout the last three years?

☐ Yes   ☐ No

(c) for periods totalling at least three years during the last 10 years?

☐ Yes   ☐ No

Leasehold information form TA7

10.1 Has the seller served on the landlord or any other person a notice under the enfranchisement legislation stating the desire to buy the freehold or be granted an extended lease?

☐ Yes   ☐ No   ☐ Enclosed
☐ To follow

If Yes, please supply a copy.

10.2 If the property is a flat in a block, is the seller aware of the service of any notice under the enfranchisement legislation relating to the possible collective purchase of the freehold of the block or part of it?

☐ Yes   ☐ No   ☐ Enclosed
☐ To follow

If Yes, please supply a copy.

10.3 Has the seller received any response to that notice?

☐ Yes   ☐ No   ☐ Enclosed
☐ To follow

If Yes, please supply a copy.

The information in this form has been given by:

Name

The Law Society

Page 6 of 6
TA7

This form is part of the Law Society's TransAction scheme.
The Law Society is the representative body for solicitors in England and Wales.
Laserform International Ltd is an Approved Law Society Supplier

© Law Society 2007

Property:	
Seller:	

These enquiries are asked on behalf of buyers. The Seller should only respond to these enquiries if they are the Landlord, the Management Company, the Managing Agent or the Residents' or Tenants' Association or are representing any of them.

TERM	DEFINITION
Ground Rent	The rent payable to the landlord by the lessee as required by the lease.
HMO	A House in Multiple Occupation as defined by section 257 of the Housing Act 2004.
Landlord	The person or company which has granted a lease over the Property to the owner of the Property.
Lessees	The owners of properties in the Managed Area.
Managed Area	The properties including the building containing the Property, together with any land, managed by or on behalf of the Landlord under the terms of the lease. Managed Areas are sometimes also called common parts.
Management Company	A management company referred to in the lease, or a Right to Manage Company created under the Commonhold & Leasehold Reform Act 2002, to provide services and administer the terms of the lease either directly or through managing agents.
Managing Agent	A person or organisation which acts on behalf of the landlord, management company or Right to Manage Company [within their terms of reference, subject to any legal restrictions].
Property	The property known by the above address, including any land and outbuildings leased to the Seller.
Reserve Fund	A fund collected from the Lessees which allows the build-up of monies to pay for repairs and the replacement of major items (such as lifts) or to equalise cyclical expenditure (such as external decoration), avoiding excessive peaks in the Service Charge. Reference to Reserve Fund includes any sinking fund or replacement fund.
Residents'/Tenants' Association	A group of some or all of the Lessees with or without a formal constitution or corporate status, or a recognised residents association which is 'recognised' by law and with a formal constitution.
Right to Manage Company	A company owned by the Lessees that manages the Managed Areas on behalf of the Landlord or Management Company, within their terms of reference, subject to any limitations.
Service Charge	The amount payable by a lessee as a contribution to the costs of services, repairs, maintenance, insurance, improvements or costs of management etc. as set out in the lease. The amount payable may vary according to the costs incurred or to be incurred.
Section 20	Section 20 of the Landlord & Tenant Act 1985, which requires the Landlord or Managing Agents to consult with the Lessees about certain proposed works.

Please complete the information requested. It is important that the incoming lessee is fully aware of their obligations so the information given must be as accurate as possible. If there is insufficient space, continue on a separate sheet.

SECTION 1: CONTACT DETAILS	Complete the details for the relevant parties or cross through if not applicable. If there are more parties involved, provide details on a separate sheet.

1.1 Landlord	1.2 Management Company
Name	Name
Address	Address
Telephone	Telephone
Email	Email

1.3 Managing Agent	1.4 Residents'/Tenants' Association
Name	Name
Address	Address
Telephone	Telephone
Email	Email
Appointed by: ☐ Management Company ☐ Landlord ☐ Other	

1.5 Who accepts service of the Notice of Assignment & Charge?

Tick the box beside each party and state the total fee including VAT for notice of assignment and charge.

☐ Landlord   £ _____
☐ Management Company   £ _____
☐ Managing Agent   £ _____
☐ Other   £ _____

If other, provide contact details for service:

Name [_____]

Address [_____]

Telephone [_____]

Email [_____]

Capacity (e.g. Landlord's lawyer) [_____]

1.6 Who collects the Ground Rent?

☐ Landlord   ☐ Management Company   ☐ Managing Agent   ☐ N/A

1.7 Who collects the Service Charges?

☐ Landlord   ☐ Management Company   ☐ Managing Agent   ☐ N/A

1.8 Who collects the building insurance premiums?

☐ Landlord ☐ Management Company ☐ Managing Agent ☐ N/A

1.9 Who deals with the day to day maintenance of the building?

☐ Landlord ☐ Management Company ☐ Managing Agent ☐ the Lessees

1.10 Who deals with the day to day maintenance of the Managed Area?

☐ Landlord ☐ Management Company ☐ Managing Agent ☐ the Lessees ☐ N/A

1.11 Who organises and administers the buildings insurance?

☐ Landlord ☐ Management Company ☐ Managing Agent ☐ the Lessees ☐ N/A

SECTION 2: TRANSFER & REGISTRATION

2.1	Is a Deed of Covenant required?	☐ Yes	☐ No	☐ Not Known

2.1.1 If Yes, confirm the costs applicable to the Deed including VAT   £ _____

2.2	Is a Licence to Assign required?	☐ Yes	☐ No

2.3 If Yes, specify requirements e.g. references, and any costs applicable to the Licence:

2.4 Are you aware of consent having been given to any alterations or additions to the Property?   ☐ Yes ☐ No

2.4.1 If Yes, provide details and copies of any consent:

2.5 Is the incoming Lessee required to take a share in, or become a member of, the Management Company?   ☐ Yes ☐ No ☐ N/A

2.5.1 If Yes, provide details of the procedure and fees:

2.6 What is the procedure and cost for obtaining a certificate in accordance with a restriction in the Proprietorship Register at the Land Registry, if applicable?

SECTION 3: GROUND RENT

3.1 What is the annual Ground Rent payable for the Property?   £ _____

3.2 Is the Ground Rent paid up to date?   ☐ Yes ☐ No

3.2.1 If No, supply details of the arrears:

Second Edition 2015

| 3.3 | What period is covered by the last demand? | From: __ / __ / _____ To: __ / __ / _____ |

4.1   How many properties contribute toward the maintenance of the Managed Area?

4.1.1   What is the current annual Service Charge for the Property?   £ _____

4.2   Is the Service Charge paid up to date for the Property?   ☐ Yes   ☐ No

4.2.1   If No, supply details of the arrears:

4.3   Is any excess payment anticipated for the Property at the end of the financial year?   ☐ Yes   ☐ No

4.3.1   If Yes, provide details:

4.4   What period is covered by the last demand?   From: __ / __ / _____ To: __ / __ / _____

4.5   In the last 12 months, has any inability to collect payments, from any party, affected (or is it likely to affect), the maintenance of the Managed Area?   ☐ Yes   ☐ No

4.5.1   If Yes, provide details:

4.6   Does a Reserve Fund apply to the Managed Area?   ☐ Yes   ☐ No

4.6.1   If Yes, confirm the amount collected from Lessees of the Property, currently held in the Reserve Fund: £ _____

4.6.2   Is the amount expected to be sufficient to cover the known Section 20 expenditure?   ☐ Yes   ☐ No

4.6.3   If No, supply details:

4.7   Confirm the date when the Managed Areas were last decorated, internally and externally.   Internally Date: __ / __ / ____ To: __ / __ / ____
   Externally Date: __ / __ / ____ To: __ / __ / ____

4.8   Within the next 2 years, are any Section 20 works proposed to the Property?
   ☐ completed but unpaid
   ☐ due
   ☐ anticipated
   ☐ N/A

4.8.1   If so, provide details of the works and the contribution anticipated from the Lessee:

4.9   Is any increase in the Service Charge over 10% or £100, whichever is the greater, anticipated in the next 2 years?   ☐ Yes   ☐ No

4.9.1   If Yes, provide details:

4.10   Are there any outstanding Service Charge consultation procedures?   ☐ Yes   ☐ No

4.10.1   If Yes, provide details:

4.11   Are the Managed Areas known to be affected by Japanese knotweed?   ☐ Yes   ☐ No

4.11.1   If Yes, provide details and a copy of any Japanese knotweed management plan in place.

4.12   Are there any: ☐ Yes   ☐ No
-transfer fees,
-deferred service charges or
-similar fees
expressed as a percentage of the Property's value payable
on an event such as resale or subletting?

4.12.1   If Yes, provide details:

SECTION 5: BUILDINGS INSURANCE

5.1   Are the buildings insurance premium contributions paid up to date for the Managed Areas including the Property?   ☐ Yes   ☐ No

5.1.1   If No, provide details of the arrears:

5.2   What period is covered by the last demand?   From: __ / __ / ____   To: __ / __ / ____

5.3   Has the premium been paid in full?   ☐ Yes   ☐ No

5.3.1   If No, provide details:

5.4   Have any claims been made against the policy during the last 3 years?   ☐ Yes   ☐ No   ☐ Not Known

5.4.1   If Yes, provide details:

5.5   Are any claims anticipated?   ☐ Yes   ☐ No

5.5.1   If Yes, provide details:

5.6   Are the Managed Areas covered by the policy?   ☐ Yes   ☐ No

5.6.1   (i) Has a fire risk assessment been completed?   ☐ Yes   ☐ No   ☐ No common parts

   (ii) Have any works recommended been carried out?   ☐ Yes   ☐ No   ☐ N/A

5.6.2   If No to either of the above, has the insurer been made aware of this and accepted the position?   ☐ Yes   ☐ No

5.7	Please confirm the date of the last buildings reinstatement cost assessment.	___ / ___ / _____		

| 5.8 | Is the insurance premium included in the service charge budget? | ☐ Yes | ☐ No |

5.8.1 If No, confirm the annual amount payable for the Property: £ _____

SECTION 6: DISPUTES & ENFRANCHISEMENT

6.1	Are there any on-going forfeiture proceedings in relation to the Property?	☐ Yes	☐ No

| 6.2 | Are there any documented unresolved disputes with the Lessees of any of the properties in the Managed Area? | ☐ Yes | ☐ No |

6.2.1 If Yes, to the extent permitted by the Data Protection Act 1998, please supply details:

| 6.3 | Have any steps been taken by anyone to enfranchise, exercise the right to manage, form a right to enfranchise or management company, extend the term of the lease of the Property or anything similar? | ☐ Yes | ☐ No | ☐ Not Known |

6.3.1 If Yes, provide details and copies of relevant documentation:

| 6.4 | Are you aware of any breach of the terms of the lease of this Property? | ☐ Yes | ☐ No |

6.4.1 If Yes, provide details:

SECTION 7: GENERAL

7.1 How many other properties are there in the Managed Area? _____

| 7.2 | Are they all leased on leases with similar terms? | ☐ Yes | ☐ No | ☐ Not Known |

7.2.1 If No, provide details:

| 7.3 | Is the building in which the Property is situated known to be an HMO? | ☐ Yes | ☐ No | ☐ Not Known |

7.3.1 If Yes, confirm that regulations applicable to section 257 Housing Act 2004 HMOs have been complied with:

SECTION 8: REQUIRED DOCUMENTS

Please provide the following applicable documents:-

8.1	The last 3 years published Service Charge accounts:	☐ Enclosed	☐ To follow	☐ N/A
8.2	Buildings insurance policy and schedule:	☐ Enclosed	☐ To follow	☐ N/A
8.3	Buildings insurance policy and schedule for the Managed Areas:	☐ Enclosed	☐ To follow	☐ N/A

8.4	Service charge estimate for the current year and details of the anticipated payments on account for the Property:	☐ Enclosed	☐ To follow	☐ N/A

8.5	Service charge estimate for the previous year for which accounts have not yet been prepared for the Property:	☐ Enclosed	☐ To follow	☐ N/A

8.6	Copies of any notices served on the Lessees under Section 20 in respect of any proposed works or any works which have not yet been paid for:	☐ Enclosed	☐ To follow	☐ N/A

8.7	Documentation relating to any forfeiture proceedings applicable to the Property:	☐ Enclosed	☐ To follow	☐ N/A

8.8	Any additional regulations or rules affecting the Property which are not contained in the lease:	☐ Enclosed	☐ To follow	☐ N/A

8.9 Any Deeds of Variation or other document varying the terms of the lease of this Property:

☐ Enclosed ☐ To follow

☐ Landlord's lawyer provides

☐ Please supply draft ☐ N/A

8.10 Any required Deed of Covenant:

☐ Enclosed ☐ To follow

☐ Landlord's lawyer provides

☐ Please supply draft ☐ N/A

8.11 Any Certificate of Compliance:

☐ Enclosed ☐ To follow

☐ Landlord's lawyer provides

☐ Please supply draft ☐ N/A

8.12 Any required Licence to Assign:

☐ Enclosed ☐ To follow

☐ Landlord's lawyer provides

☐ Please supply draft ☐ N/A

8.13	Copy of any permission to alter the Property which has been issued:	☐ Enclosed	☐ To follow	☐ N/A

8.14	Copy of any known notices served on the Lessee and documentation arising from them:	☐ Enclosed	☐ To follow	☐ N/A

8.15	Asbestos Survey for parts of the Managed Area built or converted before 2001:	☐ Enclosed	☐ To follow	☐ N/A

8.16	Fire Risk Assessment for the Managed Area:	☐ Enclosed	☐ To follow	☐ N/A

8.17	Memorandum and Articles of Association of the Management Company:	☐ Enclosed	☐ To follow	☐ N/A

8.18	Minutes of the last AGM for the Management Company:	☐ Enclosed	☐ To follow	☐ N/A

Signed	Dated ....
Print Name: .... Company:	*Please tick as applicable below, to confirm the capacity in which the answers are given.* ☐ Managing Agent ☐ Management Company ☐ Landlord ☐ Residents' Association

Note
Additional enquiries. Raise only those specific additional enquiries required to clarify issues arising out of the documents submitted or which are relevant to the management of the Property or which the buyer has expressly requested. Resist raising any general additional enquiries that can be established by the buyer's own enquiries, survey or personal inspection.

Disclaimer
Whilst care has been taken in the preparation of this form, no legal liability is accepted by the organisations which created the form. This disclaimer does not affect the legal responsibilities of the person, or organisation, completing this form to answer to the best of their knowledge and ability. If you have any queries you should discuss these with your conveyancer or solicitor.

Index

Assents, 19

Bankruptcy search, 49
Boundaries, 43, 50, 60
Buildings regulation consent, 41
Buyers Solicitor, 13

Capital Gains Tax, 22, 56, 60
Coal search, 42
Complaints handling, 32
Completion, 3, 6, 9, 37, 38, 39, 40, 53, 61, 77, 89
Consumer Credit Act 1974, 50
Co-ownership, 20
Co-Sellers, 21

Deeds of Gift, 19
Discharge of sellers' Mortgage, 11
Draft contract, 8, 63, 89

Easements, 42, 51, 63
Environmental search, 7, 39, 41, 42
Escrow, 63
Exchange Contract, 6
Exchange of Contracts, 6, 8, 9, 29, 79, 85

Financial Charges, 21
First Legal Charge, 48
First Registration, 19
Fixtures Fittings and Contents List, 21, 76
Flying freeholds, 42
Freehold absolute, 19
Freehold Possessory, 19
Freehold Qualified, 20

Good leasehold, 20
Inheritance tax, 20
Insurance, 51, 65
Insuring the property, 20

Law Society's Formulae, 29
Leasehold Absolute, 20
Leasehold Possessory, 20
Leasehold qualified, 20
Legal Costs, 52
Lender's requirements, 21

Management company, 49
Mining search, 8
Money Laundering Regulations 1993, 45

Planning, 20, 21, 22, 41, 47, 67, 68
Post-completion stage, 5
Power of Attorney, 50
Pre completion searches, 6
Proprietorship register, 42
Protocol Forms, 21, 37, 43
Purchase price, 30, 50

Radon gas search, 8
Requisitions, 6, 78, 86, 89
Requisitions on Title, 6, 78, 86, 89
Restrictive Covenants, 47

Searches, 7, 41, 46, 69
Sellers Solicitors, 13
Stamp Duty Land tax, 6
Status of the Conveyancer, 21

Taking instructions, 5
Tax and Planning Consequences, 20

The draft contract, 7
The National Conveyancing Protocol, 18
The pre-contract stage, 5
The Purchase Deed, 10
The Seller's Leasehold Information Form, 21
The Seller's Property Information Form, 21
Title, 7, 19, 37, 40, 42, 43, 46, 54, 55, 56, 57, 61, 65, 68, 69, 70, 72, 74, 87

Vacant possession, 50
Valuation of the property, 46

Water search, 7, 39, 41

****